Why things don't work
TANK

www.raintreepublishers.co.uk
Visit our website to find out more information about Raintree books.

To order:
Phone 44 (0) 1865 888112
☎ Send a fax to 44 (0) 1865 314091
▤ Visit the Raintree bookshop at www.raintreepublishers.co.uk to browse our
💻 catalogue and order online.

Why things don't work TANK
was produced by

David West 🧑‍🤝‍🧑 Children's Books
7 Princeton Court
55 Felsham Road
London SW15 1AZ

Editor: Dominique Crowley
Consultant: David Willey, The Tank Museum, Bovington, England.
www.tankmuseum.org

First published in Great Britain by
Raintree, Halley Court, Jordan Hill, Oxford OX2 8EJ, part of
Harcourt Education. Raintree is a registered trademark of Harcourt
Education Ltd.

Copyright © 2007 David West Children's Books

10 digit ISBN: 1 4062 0567 2
13 digit ISBN: 978 1 4062 0567 1

11 10 09 08 07
10 9 8 7 6 5 4 3 2 1

British Library Cataloguing in Publication Data

West, David
  Tank. - (Why things don't work)
  1.Tanks (Military science) - Maintenance and repair - Comic
  books, strips, etc. - Juvenile literature
  I.Title
  623.7'4752'0288

Printed and bound in China

Why things don't work

TANK

by David West

Contents

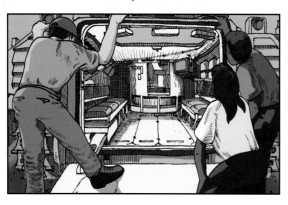
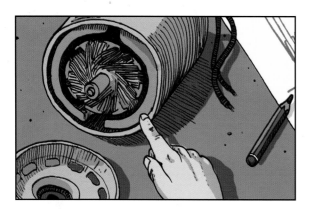
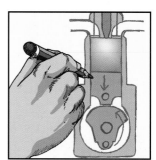

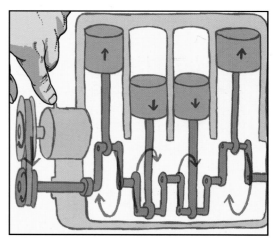

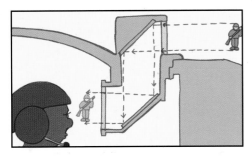

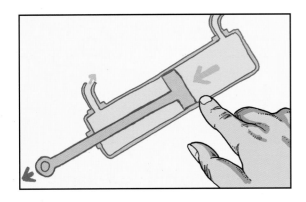

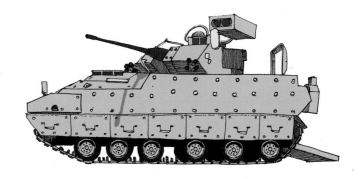

Uncle Sam's tank

JED AND JESSICA HAVE BEEN ASKED TO HELP RESTORE THEIR UNCLE'S TANK FOR HIS MUSEUM. IF THEY GET IT FINISHED IN TIME, HE WILL LET THEM DRIVE IT AROUND THE TANK RANGE. AT THE MOMENT, THERE'S A HOLE WHERE THE ENGINE SHOULD BE.

ALSO, THERE SEEM TO BE A FEW OTHER PROBLEMS...

THE BATTERIES ARE FLAT.

THE ENGINE NEEDS TO BE PUT BACK INTO THE TANK.

THE CATERPILLAR TRACK IS BROKEN.

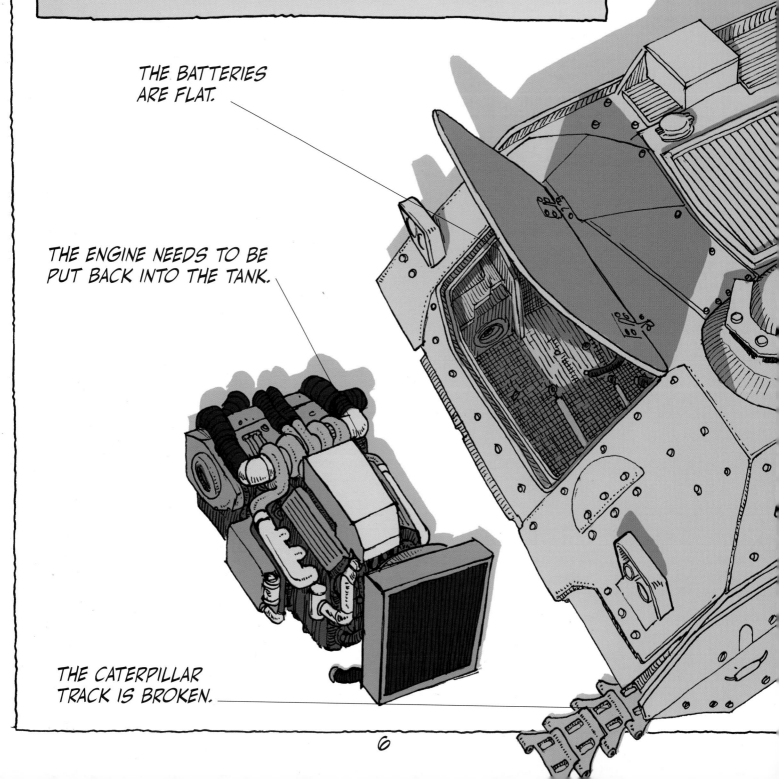

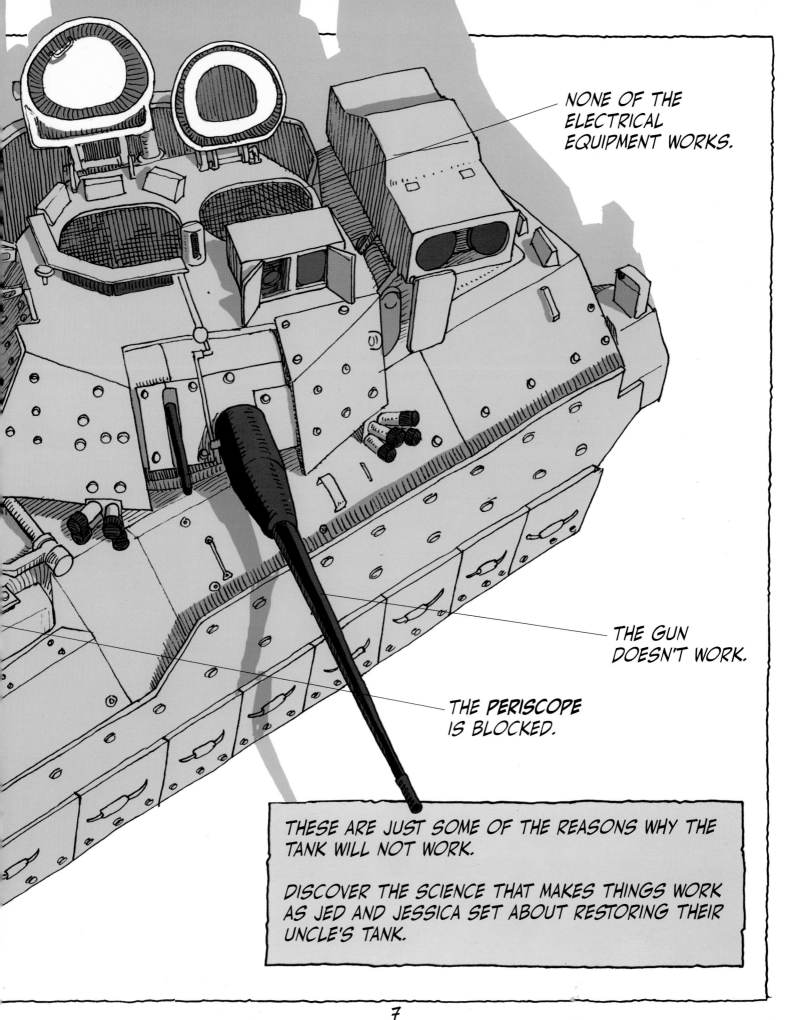

NONE OF THE ELECTRICAL EQUIPMENT WORKS.

THE GUN DOESN'T WORK.

THE PERISCOPE IS BLOCKED.

THESE ARE JUST SOME OF THE REASONS WHY THE TANK WILL NOT WORK.

DISCOVER THE SCIENCE THAT MAKES THINGS WORK AS JED AND JESSICA SET ABOUT RESTORING THEIR UNCLE'S TANK.

THERE'S UNCLE SAM WITH THE TANK.

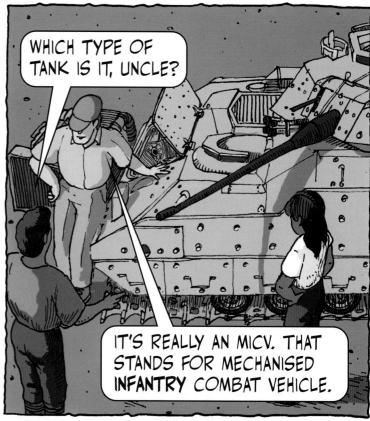

WHICH TYPE OF TANK IS IT, UNCLE?

IT'S REALLY AN MICV. THAT STANDS FOR MECHANISED INFANTRY COMBAT VEHICLE.

UNLIKE TANKS, IT HAS A COMPARTMENT IN THE BACK FOR CARRYING UP TO SIX SOLDIERS.

8

WOW! IT'S A VERY SMALL SPACE FOR SIX PEOPLE!

LOOK! IT'S EVEN GOT A TV.

YES. A CAMERA UP HERE SENDS PICTURES TO THE SCREEN. THIS ALLOWS THE SOLDIERS TO SEE WHAT IS HAPPENING OUTSIDE.

10

THE ENGINE HAS A SMALL ELECTRICITY GENERATOR, WHICH CHARGES THE BATTERIES.

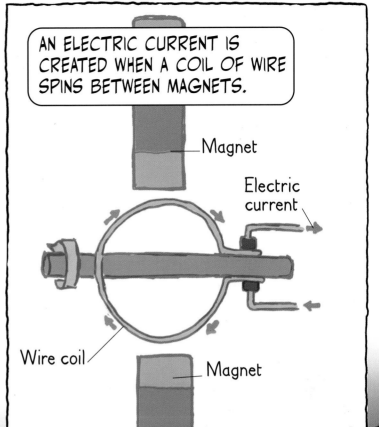

AN ELECTRIC CURRENT IS CREATED WHEN A COIL OF WIRE SPINS BETWEEN MAGNETS.

Magnet

Electric current

Wire coil

Magnet

INSIDE THIS ELECTRICITY GENERATOR, LOTS OF WIRE LOOPS ARE ATTACHED TO A SPINDLE...

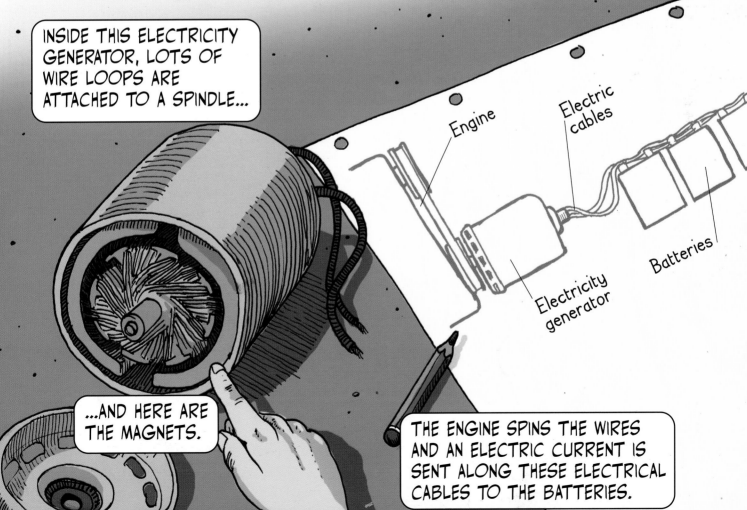

Engine

Electric cables

Batteries

Electricity generator

...AND HERE ARE THE MAGNETS.

THE ENGINE SPINS THE WIRES AND AN ELECTRIC CURRENT IS SENT ALONG THESE ELECTRICAL CABLES TO THE BATTERIES.

IT'S A VERY BIG ENGINE.

YES. IT'S A TWIN **TURBO** DIESEL.

WOW! WHAT DOES THAT MEAN?

HERE, LET ME SHOW YOU.

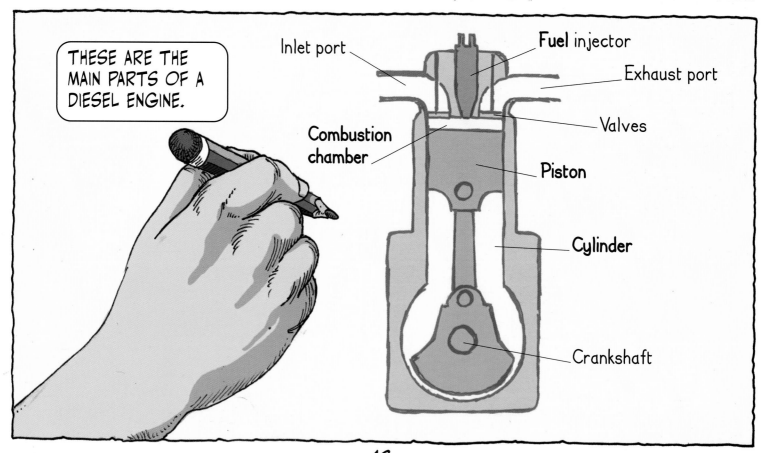

THESE ARE THE MAIN PARTS OF A DIESEL ENGINE.

Inlet port

Fuel injector

Exhaust port

Combustion chamber

Valves

Piston

Cylinder

Crankshaft

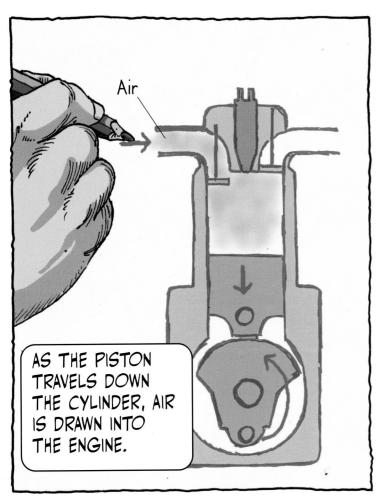

Air

AS THE PISTON TRAVELS DOWN THE CYLINDER, AIR IS DRAWN INTO THE ENGINE.

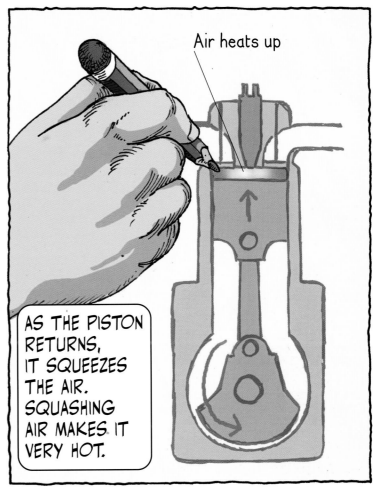

Air heats up

AS THE PISTON RETURNS, IT SQUEEZES THE AIR. SQUASHING AIR MAKES IT VERY HOT.

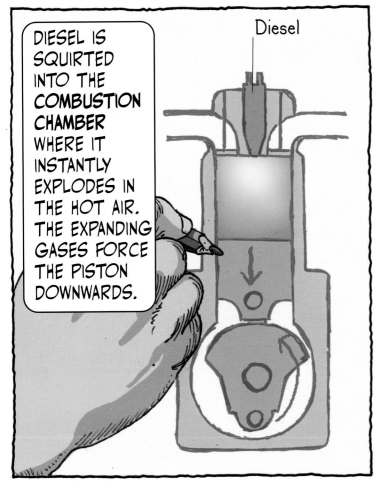

DIESEL IS SQUIRTED INTO THE **COMBUSTION CHAMBER** WHERE IT INSTANTLY EXPLODES IN THE HOT AIR. THE EXPANDING GASES FORCE THE PISTON DOWNWARDS.

Diesel

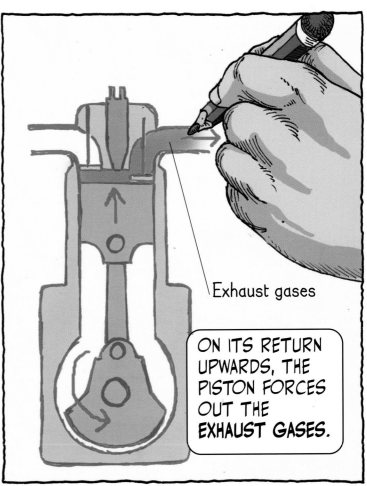

Exhaust gases

ON ITS RETURN UPWARDS, THE PISTON FORCES OUT THE **EXHAUST GASES.**

WHAT IS A TURBO?

YOU CAN GET MORE POWER FROM AN ENGINE IF YOU CAN SQUEEZE MORE AIR INTO THE COMBUSTION CHAMBER.

Air

More air

Small bang

Bigger bang

MORE AIR MEANS MORE GAS TO EXPLODE, WHICH MAKES THE ENGINE MORE POWERFUL.

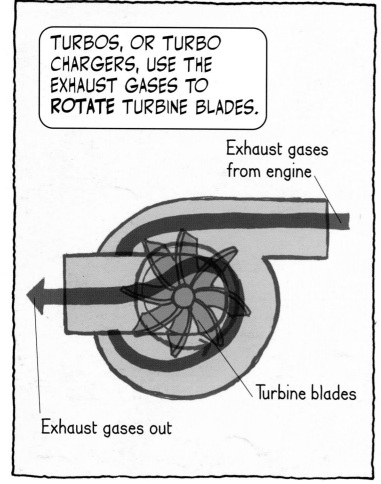

TURBOS, OR TURBO CHARGERS, USE THE EXHAUST GASES TO **ROTATE** TURBINE BLADES.

Exhaust gases from engine

Turbine blades

Exhaust gases out

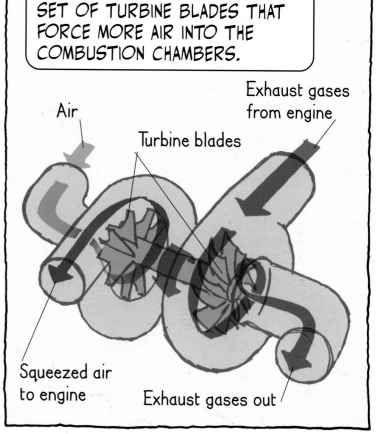

THEY ARE ATTACHED TO ANOTHER SET OF TURBINE BLADES THAT FORCE MORE AIR INTO THE COMBUSTION CHAMBERS.

Air

Turbine blades

Exhaust gases from engine

Squeezed air to engine

Exhaust gases out

YOU SEE THESE TURBO CHARGERS, HERE? THEY CAN BOOST THE POWER OF THE ENGINE BY AS MUCH AS 40 PERCENT.

LOOK. HERE COMES THE MOBILE CRANE TO LIFT THE ENGINE.

EASY DOES IT!

AFTER A WEEK'S HARD WORK, WE HAD FITTED THE ENGINE INTO POSITION.

OK. LET'S START IT UP.

CLICK

NOTHING IS HAPPENING.

OOPS. WE FORGOT THAT THE BATTERIES ARE FLAT.

THE STARTER MOTOR NEEDS ELECTRICITY FROM THE BATTERIES TO MAKE IT WORK.

HUH?

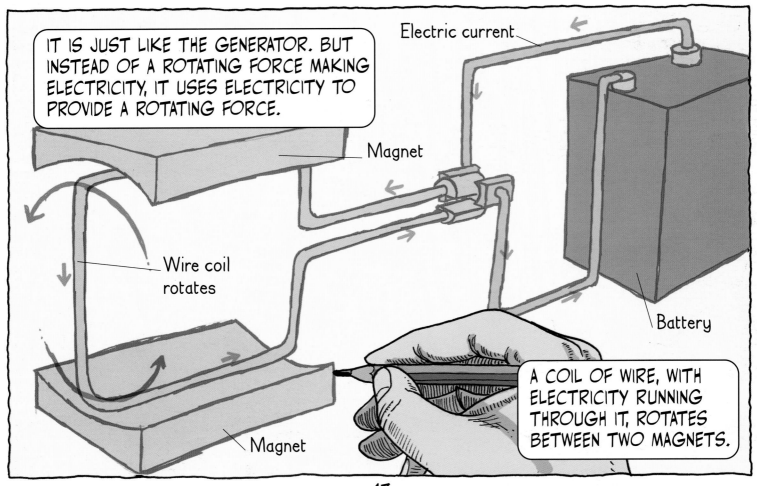

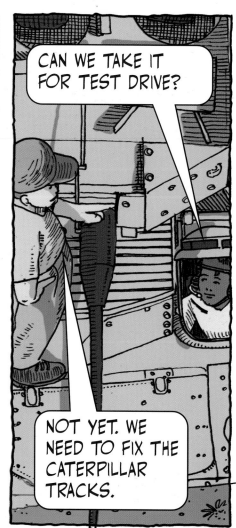

SO THAT THEY CAN MESH WITH THE DRIVE WHEELS' TEETH.

THE ENGINE DRIVES THE TWO FRONT WHEELS.

THEY MAKE THE CATERPILLAR TRACKS MOVE ROUND THE WHEELS.

THESE BITS STICKING UP KEEP THE TRACKS FROM SLIPPING OFF...

...BY FITTING BETWEEN THE SIX PAIRS OF WHEELS ON EITHER SIDE.

SO, THE WHOLE TANK RIDES ALONG ITS OWN NEVER-ENDING ROAD.

HOW DOES IT TURN?

WHEN THE DRIVER TURNS THE STEERING YOLK, IT CHANGES THE AMOUNT OF POWER TO THE TWO DRIVE WHEELS.

BY TURNING IT RIGHT, THE TRACKS ON THE LEFT GO FASTER THAN THE TRACKS ON THE RIGHT. THIS MAKES THE TANK TURN RIGHT.

IN FACT, ONE TRACK CAN GO IN AN OPPOSITE DIRECTION TO THE OTHER.

THIS CAN MAKE THE TANK VERY NIMBLE AND SPIN ROUND LIKE A BALLERINA.

WHY DO TANKS NEED CATERPILLAR TRACKS? WHY CAN'T THEY HAVE WHEELS LIKE A TRUCK?

THE ENEMY COULD EASILY SHOOT THE TYRES. A TANK NEEDS TO BE **ARMOURED**.

WHAT IF THE WHEELS WERE MADE OF METAL?

IT WOULD SINK INTO SOFT GROUND AND GET STUCK.

WALK OVER TO THAT BUSH.

YIKES! I'M STUCK.

BY PUTTING THESE PIECES OF CARDBOARD DOWN, I CAN WALK OVER THIS GROUND EASILY.

THAT'S BECAUSE I'VE SPREAD MY WEIGHT OVER A LARGER AREA. SO MY GROUND PRESSURE IS SMALLER.

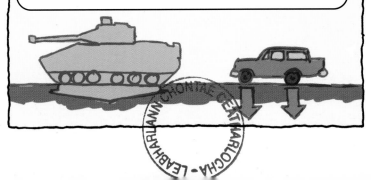

ALTHOUGH THIS TANK WEIGHS 30,000 KILOS, ITS TRACKS HELP MAKE ITS GROUND PRESSURE PER SQUARE METRE LESS THAN THAT OF A FAMILY CAR.

21

WE SOON HAD THE TRACKS MENDED.

OK. TURN ON THE ENGINE.

BRAAAAR

CAN WE TEST DRIVE IT NOW?

YES. BUT WE NEED TO BRING UP THE RAMP.

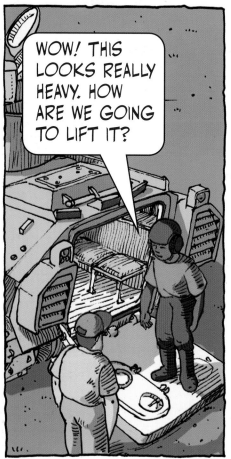

WOW! THIS LOOKS REALLY HEAVY. HOW ARE WE GOING TO LIFT IT?

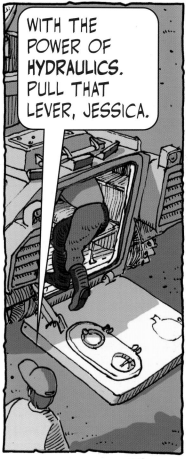

WITH THE POWER OF HYDRAULICS. PULL THAT LEVER, JESSICA.

THAT'S REALLY POWERFUL!

HMMMM

YES, HYDRAULIC POWER CAN MOVE HUGE WEIGHTS.

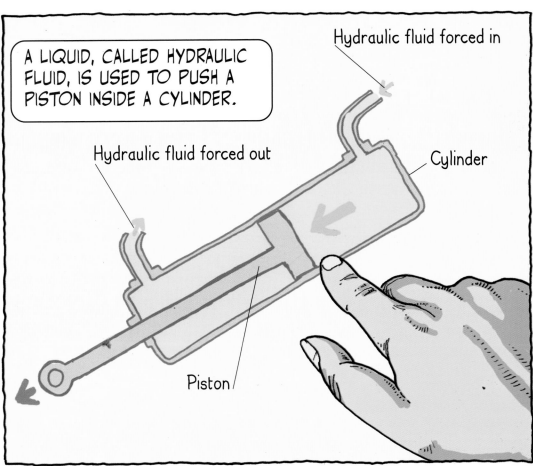

A LIQUID, CALLED HYDRAULIC FLUID, IS USED TO PUSH A PISTON INSIDE A CYLINDER.

Hydraulic fluid forced in

Hydraulic fluid forced out

Cylinder

Piston

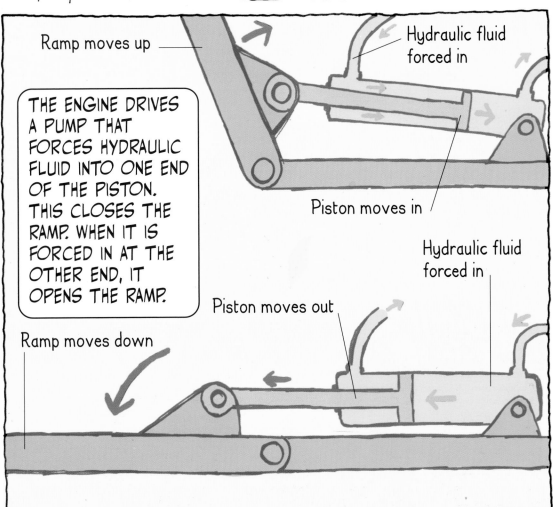

THE ENGINE DRIVES A PUMP THAT FORCES HYDRAULIC FLUID INTO ONE END OF THE PISTON. THIS CLOSES THE RAMP. WHEN IT IS FORCED IN AT THE OTHER END, IT OPENS THE RAMP.

Ramp moves up

Hydraulic fluid forced in

Piston moves in

Ramp moves down

Piston moves out

Hydraulic fluid forced in

OK. PULL DOWN YOUR **HATCH**, JESSICA.

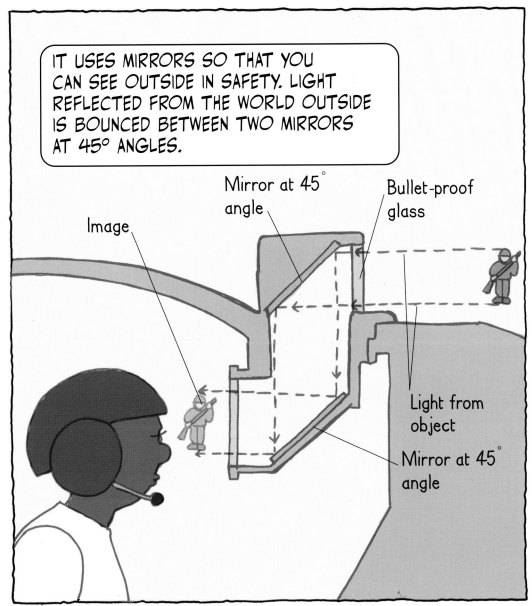

IT USES MIRRORS SO THAT YOU CAN SEE OUTSIDE IN SAFETY. LIGHT REFLECTED FROM THE WORLD OUTSIDE IS BOUNCED BETWEEN TWO MIRRORS AT 45° ANGLES.

Mirror at 45° angle

Bullet-proof glass

Image

Light from object

Mirror at 45° angle

OK, LET'S MOVE OUT.

JESSICA PRESSED THE **ACCELERATOR** PEDAL AND WE WERE OFF.

TRY TO FOLLOW THE TRACK.

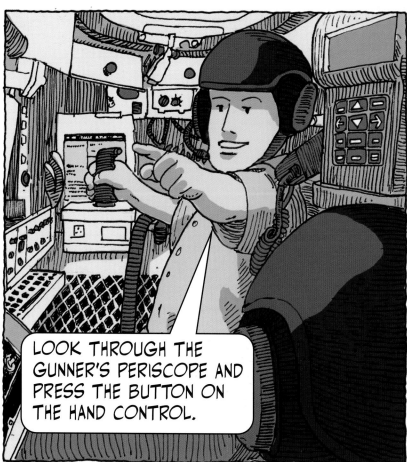

White light

Laser light

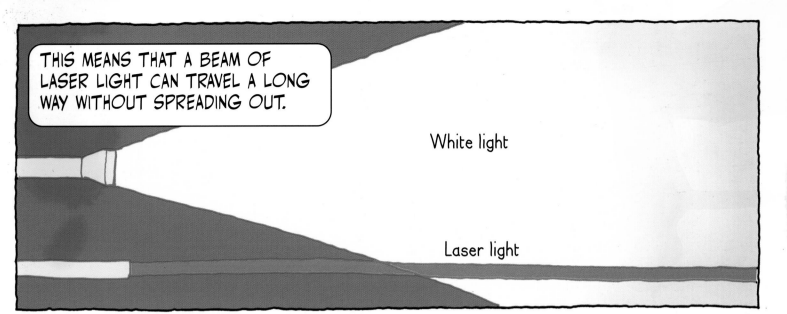

THIS MEANS THAT A BEAM OF LASER LIGHT CAN TRAVEL A LONG WAY WITHOUT SPREADING OUT.

White light

Laser light

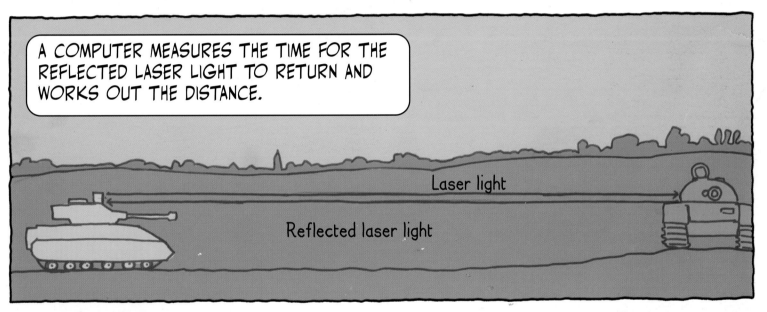

A COMPUTER MEASURES THE TIME FOR THE REFLECTED LASER LIGHT TO RETURN AND WORKS OUT THE DISTANCE.

Laser light

Reflected laser light

WHY DOES IT NEED A LASER RANGEFINDER?

THE INFORMATION IS FED INTO A COMPUTER TO CONTROL THE GUN AND **TURRET**.

Reflected laser light

Gun

Computer

WE HAD FUN TAKING TURNS TO DRIVE THE TANK AROUND, BEFORE FINALLY CLEANING IT, READY FOR THE MUSEUM'S DISPLAY.

THE NEXT DAY WE LOOKED AROUND UNCLE SAM'S TANK MUSEUM.

THIS IS WHAT THE FIRST TANKS LOOKED LIKE. THEY WERE USED IN THE FIRST WORLD WAR.

28

Parts of a tank

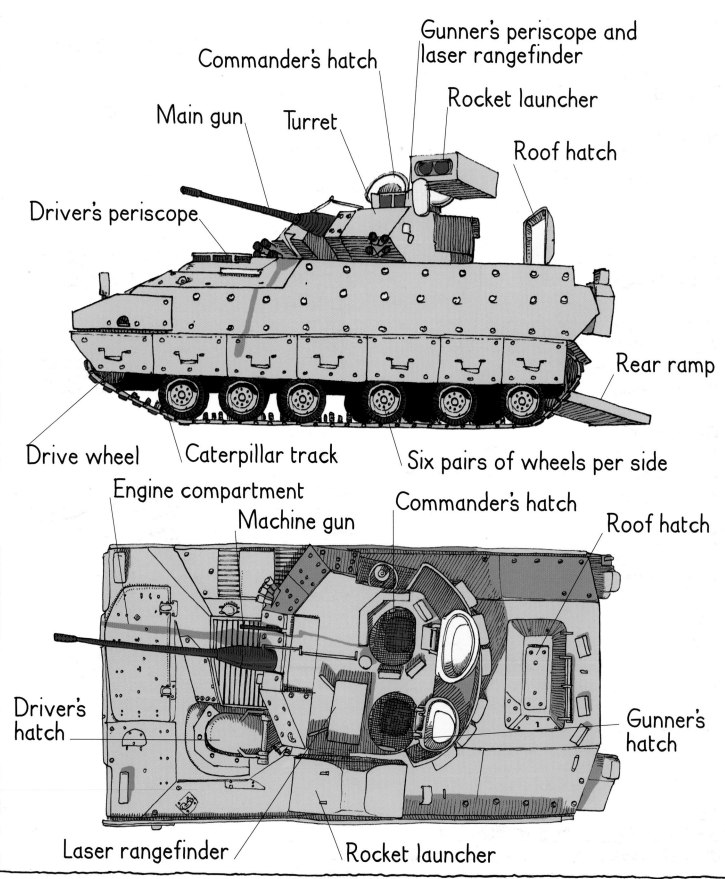

Commander's hatch

Gunner's periscope and laser rangefinder

Rocket launcher

Main gun

Turret

Roof hatch

Driver's periscope

Rear ramp

Drive wheel

Caterpillar track

Six pairs of wheels per side

Engine compartment

Commander's hatch

Machine gun

Roof hatch

Driver's hatch

Gunner's hatch

Laser rangefinder

Rocket launcher

Glossary

ACCELERATOR
THE PEDAL OR LEVER THAT CONTROLS SPEED BY CHANGING THE AMOUNT OF FUEL SUPPLIED TO THE ENGINE

ARMOUR
OUTER PROTECTIVE SURFACE DESIGNED TO WITHSTAND HOSTILE GUNFIRE

BATTERY
A DEVICE TO STORE ELECTRICITY. THE BATTERY PROVIDES POWER FOR THE STARTER MOTOR.

COMBUSTION CHAMBER
THE TOP PART OF THE CYLINDER WHERE THE FUEL/AIR MIXTURE IS IGNITED BY THE SPARK PLUG

CRANKSHAFT
A SHAFT THAT IS ROTATED BY THE UP AND DOWN MOVEMENT OF THE PISTONS IN AN ENGINE

CYLINDER
THE METAL SLEEVE INSIDE WHICH A PISTON MOVES

DIESEL
A TYPE OF FUEL THAT BURNS WHEN IT IS COMPRESSED AND IS DESIGNED TO WORK IN A DIESEL ENGINE

EXHAUST GASES
THE GASES CREATED BY THE EXPLODING FUEL/AIR MIXTURE IN THE ENGINE

FUEL
MATERIAL THAT IS BURNED TO GIVE POWER. TANK FUEL IS MADE FROM OIL.

HATCH
SMALL DOOR THAT COVERS AN OPENING

HYDRAULICS
PRESSURE APPLIED BY A LIQUID

INFANTRY
GROUP OF SOLDIERS WHO FIGHT ON FOOT

PERISCOPE
SYSTEM OF MIRRORS THAT ALLOWS VISION OVER OBSTACLES OR ABOVE EYE LEVEL

PISTON
A SOLID CYLINDER THAT MOVES TO AND FRO INSIDE ANOTHER, HOLLOW CYLINDER

ROTATE
TURN

TURBO OR TURBOCHARGER
A DEVICE WITH TURBINES (WHEELS WITH A NUMBER OF BLADES AROUND THEIR EDGES), WHICH USES THE ENERGY PRODUCED BY EXHAUST GASES TO COMPRESS AIR

TURRET
SMALL REVOLVING TOWER ON THE TOP OF A TANK

Index